How to Buy a House with Bad Credit

- Santosh Mali -

Disclaimer

All the material contained in this book is provided for educational and informational purposes only. No responsibility can be taken for any results or outcomes resulting from the use of this material.

While every attempt has been made to provide information that is both accurate and effective, the author does not assume any responsibility for the accuracy or use/misuse of this information.

Table of Contents

Preface

Welcome!

Thank you so much for buying this book. I know you will find it to be full of tremendous value. I want you to know that I do not take your purchase lightly.

Buying a house is one of the most coveted dreams in a person's life. People save all throughout their life just to be able to buy a nice, cozy home where they can spend the rest of their lives with friends and family members.

However, in today's life, buying a house is not easy, especially if you are trying to get a home loan. You need to pay a huge down payment and then get a loan for the remaining amount. And, this is applicable only if you have a lump sum amount of or have a good credit.

But, what if you don't have a good credit score or don't have a huge sum of money to give as down payment?

Does it mean that you have to let go of your dream of purchasing that beautiful home? No, definitely not! Wondering how?

Before you continue reading this report, I wanted you to download this FREE Credit Repair Manual in conjunction with this book. This will help you better

along the way. You can download it here…
http://www.freefinancialfreedom.com/free-creditrepair-manual

I recommend you download this FREE report before you continue reading this report so that you can know some extra moves with all the tips and tricks cover in this book.

Once you are done reading this book from start to finish, I have no doubt in my mind that you will know for sure that these tips and tricks help you buying a home though you have BAD CREDIT.

Alright guys, here an eBook that will help you buy a house without paying a down payment or with a bad credit score.

So, let's get started right now!

What Is a Credit Score?

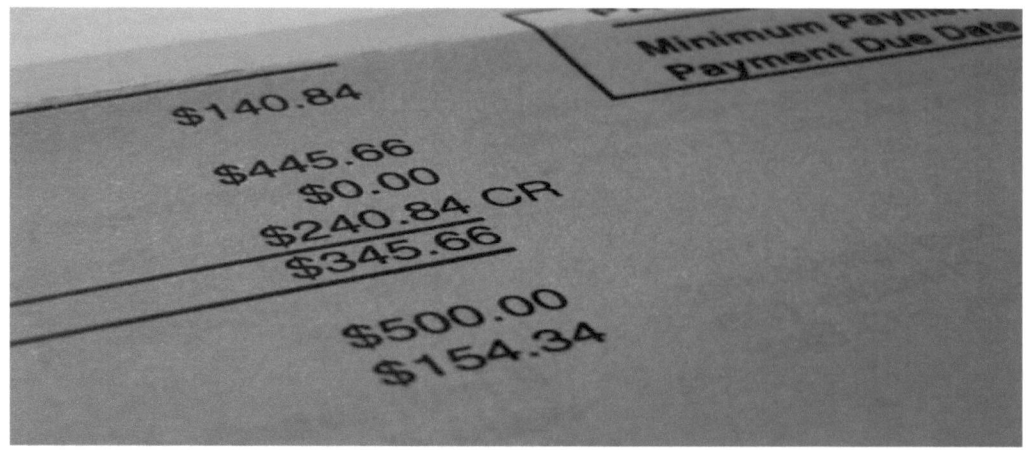

A credit score determines your creditworthiness as an individual who is seeking financial help from a bank or an institution.

This credit score is calculated based on your past transactions and how you have dealt with them. For example, let's assume that you applied for a credit card from a bank. Now, every month you use your credit card for various expenses like shopping, going to the movies, or having dinner and the bill amounts to approximately $100.

You are liable to pay this amount within a stipulated time period, beyond which the bank has the right to charge a huge interest on this amount. If you have been paying your dues regularly and have never exceeded the deadline, then you will earn a good credit score. In due course of time, the bank will increase your credit limit and also shower you with other incentives.

But on the other hand, if the bank has to constantly remind you to pay your dues and you have always come up with some excuses, then you are paving the way for earning a bad credit score. If you fail to pay once or twice due to some genuine reason, then that doesn't affect your credit score but if you make a habit out of it, then your credit scores are affected adversely.

If you have bad credit and want to purchase Auto, home or want to get credit card, see how much it will cost you...

WHAT BAD CREDIT COSTS		
IF YOU HAVE BAD CREDIT, YOU ARE PAYING FOR IT!		
$20,000 Auto Purchase	$150,000 Home Purchase	Credit Cards
Good Credit =7% $350 payments Bad = 20% or more $600 pmnts	Good Credit = 6.5% = $900 pmnt Bad = 10% = $1,400	Good = 9% Bad = 30%
Good Credit = $0 Down payment Bad = 1/3 down, $6,500	Good Credit = $0 Down Bad = 20%- $30,000 Down	Often with credit issues, you can't even rent a home for your family let alone purchase one.

This is not the case with just credit cards but can do with any financial deals that you might have made in the past.

For example, if you have been living in a rented house for a long time and you have failed to pay the rent on time, then this will give you a bad credit score.

Also, if you borrowed a loan from a bank and you haven't been able to pay the dues on time, then your credit scores will not help you in securing another loan.

Remember that every recorded financial transaction adds to your credit score. Therefore, you should make sure that you don't end up earning a bad credit history because this credit score is circulated amongst major banks and financial institutions.

Whenever you go to apply for a new loan or a credit card, your credit score will be strictly evaluated and only then you will be considered for a loan.

So, if you have just started making financial transactions, it's important that you learn to take responsible decisions in this sector and make sure that you have a high credit score.

Sometimes, you might not be able to keep track of such financial rules or you might be too busy to take notice, in such cases, it might be a good idea to hire a financial expert who can help you deal with your expenses in a better way.

However, if you have unfortunately earned a bad credit score, you still stand chances of buying that dream house of yours.

It will not be as easy as it might have been if you had a good credit score, but if you know the right tactics, then buying a house shouldn't be very tough.

Here are a few suggestions that will help you buy property when you are short of cash for down payment or have a bad credit score.

Preparing For Documents

Keep All Your Documents Ready

Not everyone gets a chance in life to build a good credit score. Sometimes, you might face unforeseen situations, which might have compelled you to make some bad financial transactions.

However, this definitely doesn't mean that you can no longer have a good life or that you have to let go off your dream of buying a beautiful house for your family.

If you are planning to buy a house with a bad credit score, you have to convince the sellers of your creditworthiness.

For example, let's assume that you had a long pending loan, which you cleared way past the deadline. And, this gave you a bad credit score. You might have faced some sudden expenses like hospital bills, or a family wedding due to which you were unable to curtail your expenses and pay off the loan.

In such cases, it is always better to be prepared for the future. You can always show documents which prove why you haven't been able to pay off your earlier loan on time or why your credit card bills were left unpaid.

For example, if you have a kid and you had to spend a lot on their education or if your spouse fell ill and a lot of money was spent in paying the hospital bills, then you can show the relevant documents to your lenders or sellers so that they are aware of your situation.

The main purpose here is to make sure that the lender trusts you and accepts your financial challenges. You should be able to prove that you will be able to pay off the home loan on time. If you have just got a new job, then it might be a good idea to wait for at least 6 months before you apply for a home loan.

Banks and financial institutions are usually skeptical about giving loans to people who have just started a new job because it doesn't imply financial security.

So, if you have waited so long to buy your new house, then there is no harm in waiting for another few months. Once you have settled into your job and you have made a certain amount of savings, then you can apply for a home loan. You can tell the lender about your job and the kind of savings you have been able to do, which will convince them of your credibility.

Also, when you are doing this make sure that you get in touch with a financial expert because they will be able to guide you through this ordeal.

Getting an expert to review your case will take off a lot of your stress and will help you breeze through the buying process. They are more acquainted with the laws and trends of the market and hence they will be able to guide you in the right direction.

However, if you don't have the money to afford one such expert, you can also settle for a real estate agent who has expertise in handling clients such as yours. You have to tell them clearly about your situation so that they can introduce you to potential sellers.

Usually, real estate agents charge a certain amount of money for showing you around and then finally getting you the best deal. It may seem like an extra expense, but it will save you a lot of time and energy, which you can utilize in other things like planning the interiors of the house and looking for budget-friendly furniture.

Talking with the lenders and explaining your situation to them is one of the safest and easiest ways of securing another home loan. But, while you are at it, don't forget to keep a check on your current liabilities and inform your lender of the same.

For example, let's say you just bought a new car and you are paying EMI on the car on a monthly basis. Now, this part of your monthly or annual expenditure and unless you have extra money, this will definitely affect your home loan's sanction.

Therefore, it's always a good idea to be honest about your current loans so that the lender is completely aware of your situation.

Also, it will not reflect well on you if the lender later finds out that you hid this important piece of information from him.

Finding an Acquaintance

You have a bad credit score and you don't have enough money to pay as down payment, but you have a spouse or sibling at home who is doing well in their job and have a good credit score. That is half of your worries solved!

A cosigner will be your best option to get a home loan when you are fighting financial battles. When you are applying for a home loan, banks will first verify your credit score and when that turns out to be bad, they will seek an explanation from you.

If you don't have the relevant papers or you simply failed to get a good credit score due to your own negligence, then your home loan application will be rejected. However, there is no need to lose hope as you can still buy your dream home and own it with pride.

If you have parents at home and if they have had a good credit score throughout their lifetime, they can become your co-applicant when you are applying for the home loan. Also, since your parents have worked longer than you have, they will have more savings than you do.

If you don't want to take financial help from your parents, then worry not because you can them off once the loan has been sanctioned. However, remember that the loan will be sanctioned in both the applicant's name. Therefore, you have to make sure that you pay the relevant amount every month to your parent so that don't feel overwhelmed suddenly.

On the other hand, if you have a working spouse then you can actually apply for the loan together. If they have a good credit score and a stable and secure job, chances are that the home loan will be sanctioned.

However, before you go ahead and take that decision, you should know that if you fail to pay the consecutive EMIs of your home loan, then your partner will have to pay the entire loan amount.

Hence, before you take this decision, you must chalk out a plan that will help you buy the house and also earn a good credit score for this financial transaction.

Remember that a co-signer is a great option but your fault will also reflect badly on their credit score.

So, before taking the plunge, think of the different possibilities and then apply for the home loan.

Choosing Potential Properties

Now that you have learned the various ways in which you can get a home loan in spite of having a bad credit score, it's time you looked for the perfect house.

However, when you are looking for a house to buy, you have to bear in mind the fact that you don't have a lot of money to be given out as down payment and your loan amount will be small since you have a bad credit score.

In such cases, you might have to compromise a little regarding the quality of the house.

For example, if you have always wanted to buy a house with a front garden and a backyard, you might have to settle for an apartment in a multi-storied building. However, this definitely doesn't mean that you can never own your dream house. You have to take a smart decision here.

Let's assume you got a loan amount of $20000 and the house you really want to buy comes at a price tag of $50000 in today's market. Obviously this house is out of your reach and now you are on the hunt for a property that can be covered within $20000.

If you find such a property which is likeable and also fits into your budget, the best thing to do would be to purchase it with the loan amount. Once you have settled into your new house and start paying the EMIs, you just have to wait till the loan tenure gets over.

Once the loan period is over, you can sell the house off at a higher price and then go ahead and purchase your dream home.

But, this requires a lot of planning and choosing the right property. The first property that you buy should have a high resale value otherwise you might not be able to fetch a large price for this house. Therefore, look for properties located in popular areas or properties which are well-furnished.

This way, you will be able to sell it at a higher value than what you bought it for. However, when you are doing this make sure that you don't miss out any of the EMI payment dates and pay off your loan diligently. This will help you improve your credit score, thereby establishing your credibility as an individual.

Also, if you require another home loan to buy the second property, then it will be easier to get a sanction because of your impressive past records.

Also, apart from this, you can also look for foreclosure houses [http://www.freefinancialfreedom.com/foreclosure-lists], which are being sold at a lesser price. Foreclosure houses are usually sold off by banks in a bid to recover their money. Auctions are organized to sell foreclosure houses and as soon as the banks meet its requirements, the bid is closed.

So, if you are lucky, you might be able to buy a very nice house at an affordable rate. For this you have to constantly be in touch with agents in different neighborhoods and also keep an eye out for "For Sale" houses in and around your area.

You can also ask your bank if they are going to organize any upcoming auction for selling foreclosure homes. This way, not only will you be able to make a good purchase but you will also get away with paying a very low down payment.

Also, when you sell this property, you will get the market value, which will be much higher than you what you paid for it initially. Therefore, this is not just a smart way of buying a house with a bad credit score, but is also an excellent investment plan.

However, when you are buying foreclosure homes, make sure that all the documents are in order and that there are no loopholes in the agreement.

Get a thorough check done for the property and only after you feel satisfied and reassured, go ahead and make the purchase.

Saving Money

If you have no money for paying your down payment, then you are obviously going through a financial crisis.

In such cases, you should plan a strict budget and stick to it.

For example, if you had been planning to go abroad for a vacation, choose a local destination instead. Find out your extra expenses and cut them all down. It will take you a few days to adjust to this budget, but at the end of it, you will thank yourself for saving so much money.

Also, since you have a bad credit score, your only chance of improving it is by showing your lenders that you are capable of saving enough money from your income. If your expenditure is greater than your income, there will be a deficit of funds and in such cases, how do you expect the lenders to believe that you will be able to pay off their debts?

Therefore, make a plan and sort out the most important expenses.

For example, make sure that you pay all your bills and rent on time, because they are important. Also, allocate a budget for food, medicines, and other day to day expenses. You can cut down a little from your vacation plans, outings with your friends, clubbing and socializing, and other not-so-important activities.

This way, you will be able to save a lot of money, which can be utilized in buying furniture for your new home or paying off the broker's commission.

Also, apart from saving money, you also need to make conscious efforts to improve your credit score. If you have a credit card, then make sure that you pay the bills before the deadline and always make it a point to invest some funds in savings. You can open a savings account or invest in various bonds so that the bank is aware of the amount of money you are saving with them.

This will give them the impression that with due course of time you will also be able to save enough money from your income to pay off their debts.

Conclusion

So, a bad credit score can be dealt with, if you have strategic planning and money-saving abilities. That dream house of yours can still be purchased with a bad credit if you implement the tricks given above.

Maintain a file containing all your expenses so that you can convince the lenders of your failure to get a good credit score due to unforeseen circumstances.

You can also get in touch with a financial expert or a good real estate agent to deal with the legal work.

Also, remember to check out foreclosure houses [http://www.freefinancialfreedom.com/foreclosure-lists] so that you can get a good home at a much lesser cost.

Lastly, make sure that you curtail expenses and save enough money to be able to accumulate the down payment amount for your next big purchase or to clear off the loan EMIs.

Getting a good credit score will take time, but with a little patience and planning, you will be to get in no time at all.

So, in nutshell you need to repair your credit. See how credit repairs can help you live a better life [http://www.freefinancialfreedom.com/how-credit-repairs-can-help-you-live-a-better-life]

Once again if you forgot to get your free credit repair manual you can download it here…
http://www.freefinancialfreedom.com/free-creditrepair-manual

I hope you have enjoyed reading this eBook and ready to get your first or second dream home without having good credit score.

Once again thanking you for purchasing this eBook and spending your valuable time with me…

If you want to write me back email me here support@freefinancialfreedom.com or head over to my website www.freefinancialfreedom.com and contact me.

www.ingramcontent.com/pod-product-compliance
Lightning Source LLC
Chambersburg PA
CBHW041624180526
45159CB00002BC/996